Audlem Remembers ...

the village fallen in WW1

Researched and edited by
Anne Draper

Audlem Remembers ...

the village fallen in WW1

**Researched and edited by
Anne Draper**

Published 2019

CanalBookShop
Audlem Mill Limited   The Wharf   Audlem   Cheshire   CW3 0DX

ISBN 978-1-9160125-0-9

Front cover:
Audlem Runic Cross War Memorial

Dedication

To my grandson Eric and all the pupils of Ruby Class, Year 5, St James School, Audlem, 2018/19.
Your futures are based on their sacrifice,
I hope you will remember them.

Anne Draper has asserted her rights under the Copyright, Designs and Patents Act 1988 to be identified as the copyright owner of the text and images in this book, unless otherwise attributed.

Subject to very limited exceptions, the Act prohibits the making of copies of any copyright work or of a substantial part of such a work, including the making of hard or digital copies by photocopying, scanning or similar process. Written permission to make a copy or copies must be obtained from the publisher. It is advisable to consult the publisher if in any doubt as to the legality of any copying which is to be undertaken.

Contents

5	Introduction and Acknowledgements
6	Audlem War Memorial
8	Hankelow Roll of Honour
9	Buerton War Memorial
10	Prisoners of war in Germany
11	Audlem St James C E School - Poems

The Fallen

15	Henry Noel **Atkinson**		59	John Frederick Charles Edmund **MacKenzie**
17	Leonard **Bailey**			
19	Richard **Bate**		61	Arthur **Morrey**
21	William **Bate**		63	Samuel **Morrey**
23	Clement John **Beeston**		65	Arthur Levi Watkin **Moseley**
25	John **Blanton**		67	Joseph **Neville**
27	William **Blanton**		69	John Henry **Purcell**
29	Ernest **Buckley**		71	John Thomas **Ratcliffe**
31	Charles Haddon **Cartwright**		73	John Henry **Richards**
33	Herbert **Dale**		75	Ernest **Roscoe**
35	William **Davenport**		77	Douglas **Shuker**
39	Alfred James **Dykes**		79	Arthur **Smith**
41	Sidney **Eaton**		81	(Frederick) Edward **Stockton**
43	Albert **Ellerton**		83	Richard William **Viggars**
45	Henry (Harry) **Gibson**		85	Frank **Walker**
47	Frederick William **Griffiths**		87	Bertie **Whitmore**
49	Thomas **Hampson**		89	Charles Albert **Williams**
51	Herbert **Hand**		91	Frederick **Williams**
53	John **Harvey**		93	George Watkin **Williams**
55	Frank William **Hobson**		95	Fred **Woodbine**
57	George **Lynes**		97	George Thomas **Woolrich**

*The War Memorial can be seen just to the left of St James Church.
In the foreground is the eighteenth century Butter Market.* [Peter Silvester]

Introduction and Acknowledgements

**Let those who come after,
see to it that their names are not forgotten.**

There were 22 countries involved in the First World War (1914-1918), including Belgium, Montenegro, Serbia, Greece, Portugal, Australia, Canada, India, New Zealand, South Africa, Italy, and Japan. Numbers vary, but about 16.5 million deaths occurred, including 6 million civilians, many from disease and famine. From the UK, 908,000 died and a further 250,000 British Soldiers suffered a partial or full amputation as a result of fighting in the First World War.

With the centenary of the Armistice in November 2018 approaching, I asked myself what these figures meant to me personally. The numbers were too much to get my head around. Each time I went into St James Church in Audlem, I passed the War Memorial with the list of those men who had died in WW1, but they were just names. It was then I decided to do some research to try to bring these men back to life, to see them as sons, brothers, and fathers, just ordinary people. In all, I researched 41 men, including some not on the Memorial, but who are buried in the cemetery with War Grave headstones, plus two brothers who were born in Audlem, but not remembered. The war memorial itself is a runic cross made of Runcorn stone, and also inside the church is an alabaster tablet; both were inaugurated in May 1920. They were created entirely through voluntary donations; a total of £320 was raised (equivalent to over £13,000 in 2019).

A display of information about the 41 men from Audlem who died in the First World War was held over Armistice weekend 2018 in St James Church. Included in it were poems written by Year 5, Ruby Class, from St James School Audlem; they were so well written and so integral to the display, that I have included them in this book. In all 233 men from the Audlem area 'answered their country's call'.

I want to acknowledge the tremendous help given by the following people and groups:

- Mark Potts and Tony Marks for their books *Where the fallen live forever* and *Crewe and Nantwich at War*, who provided a lot of information and photos to start my research;
- Audlem History Society and their archives, and in particular Celia Bloor, for her encouragement and previous research which she so kindly allowed me to use;
- Vicky Ellis and Alan Draper for their help in checking some of the online genealogical research undertaken.
- St James School Audlem for allowing me to reproduce the children's poems;
- People who provided other photos for display and publication;
- Peter Silvester at Audlem Mill Ltd for his advice and help in producing this book;
- The people of Audlem for their encouragement in putting this together;
- To the fallen, their sacrifice and that of their families paid for the peace we now enjoy. **'God promised to bless peacemakers, not peace lovers, there's a difference. Peacemakers pay the price of peace, peace lovers enjoy the benefits.'** Because of their bravery, we now enjoy the benefits of our lives.

Finally, thank you for buying this book. By doing so, you are contributing to the maintenance of our historic Grade I listed church, as all the profits from this book go to its repair fund.

I have attempted to be accurate in my research, but I have used both primary and secondary sources to compile the information. I apologise for any errors made in doing so.

Anne Draper

Audlem War Memorial
The Cross erected in 1920 in the churchyard, near the west door of St James Church.

Audlem War Memorial

"A sum of £125 has already been subscribed (unsolicited) towards the providing of a memorial to the men who have served or died for their King and country. The fund is in the hands of Rev. Canon Cotton (vicar). No decision has yet been taken as to the form of the memorial, but it is hoped something provided will be worthy of the object. No canvassing for subscriptions has been done, nor will it, the effort is entirely spontaneous." *Crewe Chronicle, 23rd August 1919*

"On Wednesday evening the Bishop of Chester dedicated, at a special service, the memorial to Audlem men who fell in the war. The memorial in the form of a cross, runic in character, is made of Runcorn stone, standing 14' 6" high. It was designed by Mr H.W. Bryan of London, the sculptor being Mrs Bridgeman of Lichfield. At the base of the memorial are Calvary steps fashioned out of solid Runcorn stone; this workmanship was executed by Mr Cliffe of Hankelow.

Along with the dedication of the memorial, a tablet of alabaster upon which the names of the fallen men of Audlem appear, was unveiled at the west end of the church. Both have been provided by voluntary subscriptions totalling £320." *Crewe Chronicle 28th May 1920*

The alabaster tablet affixed to the wall in St James Church in Audlem, with the names of 35 men from Audlem who died in the "Great War", 1914-1918. The names are also recorded on the cross in the churchyard (opposite).

Hankelow Roll of Honour

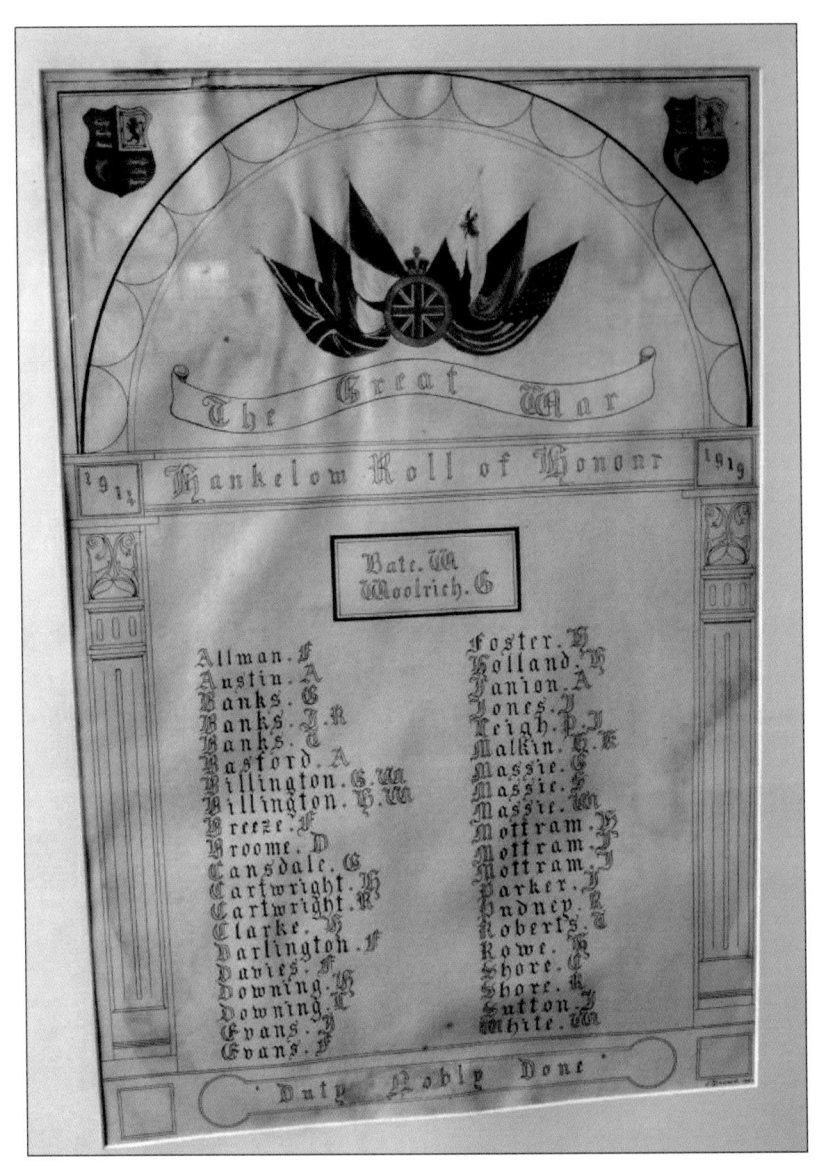

The Hankelow Roll of Honour recognises all who took part in WW1. Note however, the top box outlined in black, which shows two men from Audlem War memorial who died, who are also mentioned here:
William Bate and George Woolrich.

Buerton War Memorial

The original plaque (above), inaugurated in July 1921, was on the front face of the primary school in Buerton, but was removed after the closure and sale of the school in 2012. It can now be found in the Audlem Cemetery building. It was replaced by the monument below, sited nearby on the grass verge at the junction of Woore Road and Windmill Lane.

The names of nine of the soldiers in this book are inscribed on these memorials.

Prisoners of war in Germany

As reported in Crewe Chronicle

The following men from the Audlem area were held as prisoners-of-war during World War I:

Arthur Farrington
T. Hayes
W. Ellerton
William Tatler
Alfred Shuker
James Davenport
Charles Kendall
T. Lea
J. Povah

Alfred Shuker was imprisoned for 10 months. He stated the food was very bad until he received parcels from England. He was fairly well treated but suffered from bronchitis and dysentery.

James Davenport was imprisoned for 1 year. He stated he was taken prisoner at Cambrai on 30 November 1917. On Christmas day they had water, sand and cabbage. A few days later he and other prisoners were sent to work beyond the German lines, but they were so weak they could not work and they were thrashed and sent back to camp. The chief meals they had consisted of mangolds, turnips and potato peelings. It got better when the parcels from home got through, but cigarettes were taken away

Charles Kendall of Taintree House was captured on 15 April 1917; after nearly 2 years imprisoned, he described the disgraceful treatment by the Germans and said he would have starved but for the parcels sent from home.

Audlem, St. James' C E School

War Poems

The children of Ruby Class (Year 5 at Audlem, St. James' C.E. Primary School) tirelessly worked on producing war poems inspired by the works of North Shropshire soldier and poet, Wilfred Owen, as well as Isaac Rosenberg.

The children worked hard to incorporate elements of Anne Draper's research into their poems. In this way, we hoped to create works that allude to the real life heroes of Audlem, rather than a generic, fictitious soldier.

The poems do not rhyme, but they do feature a great many other literary devices such as metaphors, similes, personification, colloquial language, adverbial phrases and even the odd etymological reference to their chosen soldier's name.

We hope you enjoy our poems as much as we have enjoyed writing them. We are honoured to have them featured as part of this book.

Philippe Blenkiron
Ruby Class Teacher

[Wallpapers Wide]

WW1 Memorial Plaque - 'Dead Man's Penny'

The next of kin Memorial Plaque is made of bronze approx 4.5 inches diameter, with the name of someone who died serving with the British and Empire forces in WW1. (Thanks to Jeff Bryson for allowing the use of a photo of his ancestor James O. Bryson's plaque as an example). It was issued to the next of kin along with a scroll. These were posted separately, typically in 1919 and 1920. 1,335,000 were issued. No rank was stated to avoid any distinction being made between those who had paid the 'ultimate sacrifice'.

Deaths in the period 1919-1920, and maybe even later, could still lead to the presentation of the plaque, if the death was accepted as war-related. It is thought however that many war dead had no plaques or scrolls issued, due to the inability to trace addresses for eligible next of kin; this might be because of the high incidence of short term rented addresses, or if they died unmarried and their parents were dead, there might be no dependents claiming a pension.

The design of the plaque was the result of a competition, held while the war still raged, although manufacture did not start until 1919. In 1917 a committee set up the competition for any British-born person to design a plaque to record the name of a fallen service man or woman from the British and Empire forces. There were more than 800 entries to the competition from within the United Kingdom, from countries in the British Empire and from the theatres of war. The winning design was by Mr Edward Carter Preston (1894-1965). His initials, E.CR.P, appear above the foot of the lion.

The design features the figure of Britannia facing to her left and holding a laurel wreath in her left hand. Underneath the laurel wreath is a box where you will find the commemorated service person's name. The name was cast in raised relief on each plaque, achieved by a labour-intensive process not fully known today. In her right hand Britannia is holding a trident. Representing Britain's sea power there are two dolphins each facing Britannia on her left and right sides. A growling lion stands in front of Britannia, with another much smaller lion under its feet, biting the German Imperial eagle.

The Fallen

[Stephen Benson, www.cheshireroll.co.uk]

Tablet inside Audlem Church,
referring specifically to Atkinson

Resiting of Henry Atkinson's memorial in France,
October 2017 [Celia Bloor]

Henry Noel Atkinson

He used to see lands of flowers,
now he hears screams of pain.

Golden bees are stinging him in the trenches.
He was born as the snow danced in the wind,
Now his skin is as pale as the Christmas snow.

As the bombs stamp on the muddy floor,
Henry might not survive this war.

His father prays for his life in Heaven.
Born on the 25th, he only had 25 years.

Henry Noel Atkinson

Born	25 Dec 1888 at Audlem Vicarage
Enlisted	12 March 1913
Died	22 Oct 1914 Battle of La Bassee, Violaines, France
Age at death	25
Height	N/A
Chest measurements	N/A
Job	1911 A gentleman gardener
Lived at	1891 Audlem Vicarage, 1901, Heswall, 1911 Highfield Hall, Northop.
Father	Arthur (Rev. Canon)
Mother	Ursula Mary Cotton- Jodrell
Family	1 half brother George Walter Hillyard from mother's first marriage
Regiment	Following training in Londonderry with the 1st Battalion, he was deployed to France on 14 August 1914 with his original 3rd bat. Cheshire Regiment, as a Second Lieutenant he received DSO. The citation reads: 'for conspicuous gallantry under heavy fire from both flanks by collecting a few men and checking the enemy, thereby facilitating the retirement of his comrades.'
	He survived fighting at Mons, Le Cateau and the Aisne, but was reported missing, believed captured at Voilaines, Pas de Calais, on 22nd October 1914 (his father died two days later, knowing only that he was "missing"). He was promoted to Lieutenant on 2 February 1915 while still presumed missing. The Battalion War Diary for 22 October 1914 states:
	5.10 a.m. Enemy made heavy attack, and took the trenches at the point of the bayonet. Battalion retired to RUE DU MARAIS under very heavy fire. Manchesters came up in support.
	8.0 p.m. Battalion withdrawn and went in bivouac at last E of RUE DE BETHUNE.
	*Casualties: Captains Shore, Rich, Hartford, **2/Lieuts Atkinson**, Leicester, Greenhalgh missing, Captain Forster, 18 N.C.O.s & men wounded, 200 N.C.O.s & men missing including Sergeant Major.*
Buried/ remembered	Cabaret-Rouge British Cemetery, Pas de Calais in 1923, after his body was found and identified by his disc.
Other information	Schooling at Moorland House, Heswall, then at Charterhouse where he played in the 1st XI cricket team, as well as taking part in House football and winning the 1907 House Racquets Cup with Hugh Leatham (a Captain in the Royal Army Medical Corps who survived the Great War). He was also part of the school's fire brigade during the Oration Quarter of 1907 and a school monitor in his final year at the school. Upon leaving Charterhouse, Atkinson went up to St John's, Cambridge. Member of Chester golf club - won the Welsh Amateur Golf Championship 1913 on 38th hole.
	Left nearly £3000 to his mother.
	After the War, as no grave could be found, the family had a tombstone laid where it was believed he had fallen.
	In 1923 the body was found and reinterred in Cabaret Rouge British Cemetery (Grave XIII. E. 12) because it was still accepting burials. The Cheshire Regiment had the redundant stone moved to Violaines Communal Cemetery, adding the inscription:-
	"In February 1923 his body (identified by his disc) was found, together with that of an unknown soldier of the Cheshire Regiment, about 400 yards from where his stone was originally erected in a neighbouring field. Both were removed under direction of the Imperial War Graves Commission, to the Cabaret Rouge British Cemetery, Souchez. Removal of the stone having therefore become necessary it has passed into the possession of the Cheshire Regiment and has been re-erected in this cemetery as a perpetual memorial to all others of the Regiment who are still among the missing".
	In 1995 the Cheshire Regiment restored it, and repainted the weathered inscription. He is also remembered on the Northop memorial and in a window in Chester Cathedral, as well as a tablet to him alone in Audlem church.
	On 22 October 2017, the memorial to him was relocated by French volunteers to a memorial garden.

[Stephen Benson, www.cheshireroll.co.uk]

Leonard Bailey

He was as strong as a lion, now he is a scared cat.

The mean tanks are lumbering slowly
The enormous, revolting, rats eat the dead.
And the men shake like the engine of a car.
Only God knows who will go when he steps into No Man's Land.

The sorrow.
Disgraceful, deadly Germans shoot their golden bees at him
But he is a gun with good aim
BOOM
CRASH
The ghastly smell takes me back to when he was alive.
His eyes were oceans about to explode with tears
The lovely food from his grocer's shop has turned into a hard stale biscuit
HIS MEMORY IS DANCING IN THE WIND.

Leonard Bailey

Born	1894 Audlem
Enlisted	Sent to France 18 Dec 1914
Died	3 Oct 1915, Battle of Loos
Age at death	21
Height	*Not available*
Chest measurements	*Not available*
Job	Grocer's errand boy in 1911
Lived at	Little Heath
Father	James
Mother	Emma
Family	3 brothers - Charles, Herbert & Arthur
Regiment	2nd Bat. Cheshire Regiment, 10226 Private
Buried/ remembered	Loos memorial, Pas de Calais, France
Other information	Member of church choir. Memorial service held at Audlem Methodist church late Oct 1915.
	In 1911 he lived with his mother, 3 brothers, niece, aunt and a boarder in 5 rooms

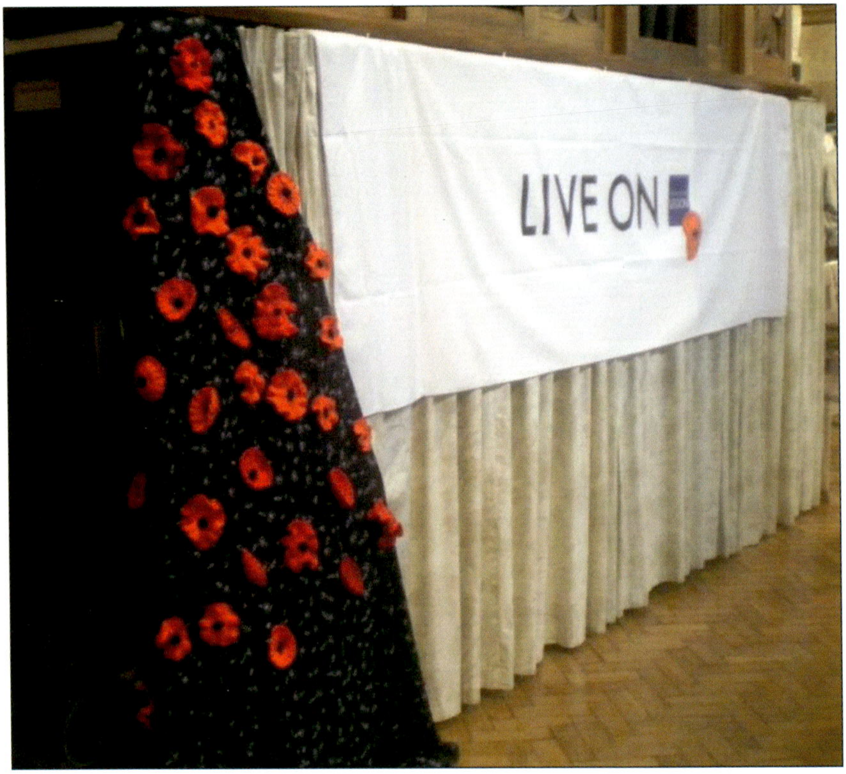
LIVE ON

Richard Bate

Born	Q2 1892 Nantwich or Whitchurch 1891/2?
Enlisted	*Not available*
Died	*Not available*
Age at death	*Not available*
Height	*Not available*
Chest measurements	*Not available*
Job	*Not available*
Lived at	1901 in a van in fox yard Northwich? Culcheth?
	1911 R Bates recorded in Cheshire regiment at Chester Castle, age 19, born Crewe.
Father	Richard?
Mother	Alice Nee Cooke?
Family	1 sister?
Regiment	There are 6 Richard Bate military records but the link to any of them cannot be established.
Buried/ remembered	*Not available*
Other information	Richard has proved very difficult to trace or to establish any link to Audlem

William Bate

William Bate was used as bait
for German fish.
His hometown doesn't sleep
while his heartbeat is still alive.

The rifles are shouting,
the bombs are screaming.
Like a dog, he dug into the ground,
tunnelling towards the creeping creatures.

The shell fell down as fast as a leopard.
It blew up as bright as the hot sun.
His eyes are camouflaged
against the mud.

———————

His feet are screaming in pain

Metallic biscuits and stale old bread was his war diet

He was the joker in a pack of cards,

A determined protector by name

A comedian to his mates

A wolf cub leading a pack of eight siblings.

He tunnelled like an ant to the centre of the world

And an uncaring shell made it his permanent home.

William Bate

Born	15 Aug 1897, Nantwich
Enlisted	Shrewsbury 1914
Died	30 June 1916
Age at death	19
Height	*Not available*
Chest measurements	*Not available*
Job	1901 Cox Bank; 1911 Cow Boy at Brown Bank Farm, Audlem, age 13
Lived at	Family lived at Lock House Audlem, and in Hankelow
Father	George Bate – lock keeper
Mother	Elizabeth Stubbs
Family	4 sisters and 3 brothers
Regiment	17th Service Bat. Manchester Regiment (2nd Manchester Pals). Private, 42195 attached to 2nd Tunnelling Co, Royal Engineers.
Buried/ remembered	Ramparts Cemetery, Lille Gate, Ypres
Other information	Killed when a shell fell among his working party, together with 11 other casualties. The letter from his captain stated 'he was quite popular amongst his comrades'.

Part of the displays in St James Church, Audlem, over the weekend of the 100th anniversary of the Armistice in November 2018.

Clement John Beeston

Born	Aug 1896, baptised 9 Aug 1896 in Audlem
Enlisted	Glasgow
Died	12 July 1915 Gallipoli
Age at death	20
Height	*Not available*
Chest measurements	*Not available*
Job	Errand boy for Chemist in 1911 census
Lived at	1896 Green Lane Audlem, and Cox Bank
Father	Clement John Beeston
Mother	Sarah Anne
Family	3 brothers Harry, George and Fred.
Regiment	'C' Company 1/7th bat. Highland Light Infantry – Private 3034
Buried/ remembered	Helles Memorial, Turkey
Other information	1911 census lived in '3 down, 2 up' house.

12 July 1915 - Battle of Achi Baba Nullah details: 157th Infantry Brigade, who had been waiting all day in the hot sun with little water and under artillery fire, followed their artillery barrage, the pipers leading 6th and 7th Highland Light Infantry in the advance, 5th Argyll and Sutherland Regiment in support. As with 155th Infantry Brigade, 157th Infantry Brigade were also successful in clearing the second line trenches and became confused looking for the non-existent third line. All battalions suffered extremely heavy casualties for little territorial gain. Some killed by 'friendly fire'.

Memorial plaque from the Macclesfield Industrial School (also known as the "Ragged" School). The Blanton brothers are commemorated on this plaque of former pupils/inmates who gave their lives in the service of their country. *[S Davies]*

John Blanton

His dirty mouth got him nowhere but trouble,
A target for Germans and mosquitos.
His eyes were as grey as the bombs
and the great ashes flying in the air.

His feet are as dirty as his rifle.
The biscuits are as hard as rock
and the soup is a dirty puddle.

The bullets are speeding through No-Mans-Land
ready to eat the square heads' flesh.
The trees stood watching there
burnt like a soldier's heart.

The stew is like glue, hard and lumpy.
The vicious rats feed on the bodies of dead soldiers
Rifles shouting with rage and anger
Dreadful bed bugs plotting quietly
Vicious guns demolishing relentlessly
Merciful trenches drinking silently

His eyes are as clear as a window pane, I can almost
see his soul, fear and devastation.
He's a still river washing the beds of the trenches
His scar is round and dirty, a broken unlucky coin.
His shoes are pulling him to No-Mans-Land and leading him to safety.

John Blanton

Born	29 October 1888 in Audlem, baptised 14 Nov
Enlisted	Feb 1909, Macclesfield. Went to France Jan 1915
Died	9 April 1915, Ypres.
Age at death	26
Height	5'5" Weight -121lbs
Chest measurements	32". Fresh complexion, grey eyes, dark brown hair. Circular scar on right side of neck and hips. Indistinct tattoo marks on left forearm.
Job	On enlistment – farm labourer
Lived at	12 March 1894 Cox Bank, enlisted at St James School. 1895 Salford. 1901 Resided at the Industrial 'ragged' school in Macclesfield after death of his father. There he was a scholar and trainee shoe maker. Left in 1904 and worked for Mr Roberts of Higher Fence Farm for a few years.
Father	William
Mother	Sarah
Family	1 brother William, 3 sisters, Lillian Linda, Sarah Ann & Ann
Regiment	2nd Bat. Cheshire Regiment, Private 9170
Buried/ remembered	Macclesfield war memorial, buried Contay
Other information	In India for 4.5 years on duty, at Secunderabad and Jubbulpore. Suffered from tonsillitis in June 1910 and had tonsil removed. In hospital in 1912 and Nov 1914 suffering from Malaria. Was disciplined on numerous occasions for swearing at an NCO; dirty rifle; lateness; slackness on duty; not firing when ordered to; creating a disturbance in regimental library and damaging a regimental tapestry; gambling outside the Company's bungalow; not getting out of bed when ordered to. Regiment returned to Devonport on 24 Dec 1914 and sent to Le Havre 17 Jan 1915. He received gunshot wounds to his chest and abdomen and suffered from gas effects. Soldiers effects, plaque and scroll given to his sister Lillian Linda Sheldon.

Depiction of Distinguished Conduct Medal bravery [Mark Potts]

William Blanton

His hair is like the muddy water that fills the trenches.
His eyes are storms of sadness, fearing he is the next to go.
His scar is a memory reminding him of the people
relying on him at home.
His mole is a volcano ready to erupt with anger!

Shock filled William's eyes like ripples on a pond.
His shoes pulled him towards No Man's Land,
to help a friend in need, to save them from the iron burning bee.

William Blanton

Born	27 July 1891 Audlem - baptised 29 July
Enlisted	6 Jan 1909 Macclesfield, posted Basra Nov 1916
Died	11 April 1917 in Mesopotamia; had been injured in January then returned to active duty.
Age at death	25
Height	5'4" Weight 134llbs; mole on right shoulder; small scars on both elbows.
Chest measurements	36". Complexion sallow, eyes grey, hair dark brown.
Job	Shoemaker
Lived at	20 May 1895 Salford, attended St James School. 1901 in Audlem workhouse after death of father. Then sent to Industrial 'ragged' school Macclesfield as child
Father	William
Mother	Sarah
Family	1 brother John, 3 sisters Lilian Linda, Sarah Ann & Ann
Regiment	8th (Ser) Bat. Cheshire Regiment, Sergeant 9140
Buried/ remembered	Basra Memorial
Other information	Accident on duty in Belfast in 1910 leaving 2" wound to shin. April 1910 offence of stealing a comrade's property; court marshal sentenced him to 84 days hard labour and discharge with ignominy. This was commuted to detention in Dublin detention barracks until June and discharge was rescinded under special order.
	Posted to Jubbulpore India in 1911, suffered from Malaria in 1912/13. Returned to Devonport Dec 1914, landed at Le Havre 17 Jan 1915.
	In June 1915 the Macclesfield Courier reported he had received the Distinguished Conduct Medal in June 1915 for 'act of gallantry and devotion in the field in going out to the rescue of a wounded man lying in the open. Being unable to move him Private Blanton remained with the man until assistance arrived, during which time he was continuously fired on ' at Moolenacker Farm Ypres France on 21st Feb 1915. It also quoted from a letter he wrote:
	Private W Blanton, who is wounded and in the Military Hospital at Barnstaple, writes to Mr W Swaine, Secretary of the Industrial School: "I expect you will be pleased to hear that I have been awarded the Distinguished Service Medal. I received a letter from my regiment to say that my name had appeared in Brigade Orders for it. I got it for bringing in a wounded man to safety from between our trench and the Germans at Ypres. I went out yesterday for the first time for a motor drive, and I enjoyed it immensely. I am getting quite well now, and it won't be long before I am discharged and back in the firing line again..."
	Soldier's effects returned to his sister Lillian Linda Sheldon.

[Celia Bloor]

Ernest Buckley

Born	1890
Enlisted	Shrewsbury. Sent to France 22 May 1915
Died	9 April 1917, Battle of Arras
Age at death	27
Height	*Not available*
Chest measurements	*Not available*
Job	Railway worker in Widnes in 1911
Lived at	Shropshire Street & Green Lane, Audlem.
Father	William Buckley
Mother	Mary Ann Hand
Family	None
Regiment	5th bat. Kings Shropshire Light Infantry – Private 10826
Buried/ remembered	Arras Memorial, Pas de Calais
Other information	Killed by an exploding shell. His commanding officer wrote: 'He was a really good soldier and willing to do anything he was told. He was always ready to do anyone a good turn.'
	Battles Of Arras - First Battle Of The Scarpe - 09/04/1917 - The Harp/Telegraph Hill (Chemin du Telegraphe). Allied victory, part of a large Allied offensive to break through German front lines and attack reserves of troops and materials. British advanced before dawn and through inclement (sleet, snow, strong winds) weather.

Charles Haddon Cartwright

Charles Haddon Cartwright

Born	Q3 1892
Enlisted	11 Dec 1915, Chester; mobilised 9 Jan 1917 to Army Service Corps, Bath
Died	15 November 1918 in Audlem after discharge due to ill health - 'diabetes aggravated by active service'.
Age at death	26
Height	5'5"
Chest measurements	35.5"
Job	Baker for John Wood of Victoria House, Audlem
Lived at	Hankelow
Father	Joseph
Mother	Mary A
Family	3 brothers, 2 sisters
Regiment	290433 Private in ASC. 23 Feb 1917 to the 1st Training Battalion as Private TR/1576. On 31 May 1917, he was posted to join the British Expeditionary Force in France, transferred as Private 36883 to the 1st Northumberland Fusiliers. On 2 July 1917, he was posted to the Northumberland Fusiliers Depot. On 30 August 1917, he was medically discharged as being no longer physically fit for war service.
Buried/ remembered	Audlem Cemetry, row 21, grave 283
Other information	Received British War and Victory medals.

[Mark Potts]

Herbert Dale

His feet are screaming in pain in muddy, dirty water.
The biscuits are as hard as metal, and the jam is as sticky as the mud.
The trenches slowly swallowed the soldiers,
The guns are alive and are assassinating them,
The trees are tripping over the rocks.

His first job was fighting in the war,
21 years old, with dark black hair
And a round nose like a mole.
Herbert, bright army, in a regiment covered in mud.
The flying sting-ray stung his brain,
And his blood grew into poppies.

Herbert Dale

Born	1897, baptised 17 March 1899 in Audlem
Enlisted	Crewe
Died	20 Sept 1918, Flanders, France
Age at death	21
Height	*Not available*
Chest measurements	*Not available*
Job	*Not available*
Lived at	1901, Copthorne, Audlem; 1911, Lightwood Green in 4 rooms
Father	Robert Dale
Mother	Mary Ellen
Family	4 brothers & 3 sisters
Regiment	3rd bat. Worcestershire Regiment – Private 43177 Formerly 44608 South Lancs Regiment.
Buried/ remembered	Le Touret Cemetery, Pas de Calais, France
Other information	Shot in the head during battle Mother granted war gratuity 13 Nov 1918, revised 17 Dec 1919.

William Davenport

The biscuits are as hard as titanium.
The soup is left to go ice cold.
His feet are screaming to go home and out of torture.
He was cramped before
now he's claustrophobic.

He cut wheat back on the farm, and when he came back
he cut *himself down*.
At the end, his port leaked out of his body,
As he thought of the deadly iron bees draining the soldiers' honey.

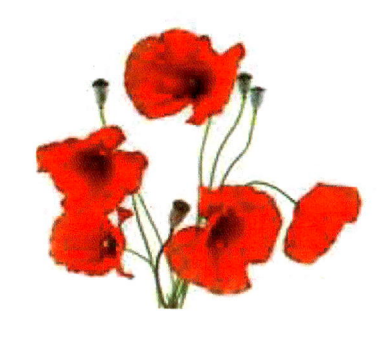

William Davenport

Born	1876 Audlem
Enlisted	Chester
Died	16 March 1917
Age at death	41
Height	*Not available*
Chest measurements	*Not available*
Job	1891 General servant, Hankins Heys
	1901 & 1911, Farm labourer
Lived at	1881 Chapel End, 1901 Kynsal,
	1911 & 1914, Kynsal Heath,
Father	John, committed to Chester Asylum 1890s
Mother	Sarah A
Family	3 brothers, 3 sisters.
	Married to Annie, 13 years younger than him;
	1 daughter Sarah Ann, born 1907
Regiment	Welsh regiment 54614 Private & 58th Bat Training Reserve TR4/5367 Private
Buried/ remembered	Buried Audlem Cemetery, row 17 grave 267.
Other information	1911, lived with 2 brothers, his wife, daughter & 5 other relations in 7 rooms.
	Committed suicide - see newspaper article.
	His effects left to his wife £5, 3 shillings 6 pence.

William Davenport

Soldier's Sad End: the Inquest

Crewe Chronicle - 24 March 1917

On Monday an inquest was held by Mr J.C. Bate (West Cheshire Coroner) at the police station Audlem, on the body of **Private William Davenport** whose home was at Kynsal Audlem. The deceased was aged 41, and was a general labourer and was in the 58th A.R.B. Cheshire Regiment, and had been until Wednesday 14th inst, at Kinmel Park, North Wales. He joined the army on 24th August 1916 and was put in the Labour Battalion and had been in training in Wiltshire and Kinmel Park.

On Wed 14th inst. he was removed to Chester and came home about 9.30pm on Thursday without leave, but told his wife Annie P Davenport it didn't matter if he got back by 9am on Friday. At 5.20am on Friday he left on his bicycle for Crewe Station. She tied his army coat on the carrier of his bicycle and he got the bicycle ready before starting. He had to get to Crewe sometime about 7 to catch the train to Chester.

He was billeted out, did nothing there except go out for a march in the morning. She heard nothing of him that day, but expected a letter from him on Saturday as he promised to write. She heard of him that afternoon, and saw his body at the Bridge Inn.

Before leaving home he shaved. He brought a razor with him and took it back with him. It was the razor produced.

He was bright and cheerful when he left, and did not complain of being short of anything. He didn't like being at Kinmel Park. He was 41 four days after he joined the army. He didn't tell his wife why he had been removed, but said they were going to be medically re-examined at Chester. He was put in Class C2 about a month ago. He didn't like the idea of being Class A and going to France. He had been in Class A and was afraid he'd be put in it again.

His wife said he never threatened to take his own life. She never thought he might do so and had no suspicion of it when he left home.

P.C. Skilbeck stated that he was a constable stationed at Audlem. On Saturday morning he received notice that there was some clothing and a bicycle lying on Longhill Moss. He went there, and found an army overcoat, tunic and cap lying on a bicycle, which was lying flat on ground on the far side of the Moss. On searching the Moss in a shallow pit, about 50 yards from the bicycle, he found the body of the deceased just covered with water, lying on his back with the hands lying on the breast. In the trouser pocket he found a purse containing 8s 5d. The deceased's throat had been cut, the windpipe being severed. Deceased's wife identified the body in his presence.

Later a man named Rycroft handed witness a razor and case found a few yards from where the bicycle lay, and near a pool of blood behind some bushes about 50 yards from the pool.

The deceased father had been in Chester County Asylum 20 or 30 years. One brother resided at Audlem and two were in the army.

The jury returned a verdict that deceased committed suicide by cutting his throat with a razor, but there was not sufficient evidence to show the state of his mind at the time he committed the act.

[S McKinnell]

Albert James Dykes

His home was a trench invaded by square heads…
In his memory, the juicy tomatoes smelt like victory
Now, the hard biscuits smelt of nothing,
just the shame of No Man's Land.

His hair was like the muddy dirt that filled the trenches.
His skin is as pale as the mustard gas that fills the air.
No Man's Land is a death trap leaving eternal death…
I see his soul crying for help, screaming his name…

It didn't have to be like this…

Albert James Dykes

Born	Buerton, 6 Aug 1878
Enlisted	Joined Royal Marines Band 10 Nov 1899, went with band to France in 1916.
Died	28th December 1917, Gosport Hospital, from erysipelas and septicaemia from injury to finger.
Age at death	39
Height	5'6"
Chest measurements	*Not available*. Fair complexion, light brown hair, blue eyes, mole on head
Job	Grocer's assistant
Lived at	Chapel End & School Lane, Audlem
Father	James Dykes
Mother	Elizabeth Gater
Family	1 brother & 2 sisters – Annie May lived in Audlem for many years.
Regiment	Royal Marine Band – musician PO/10210
Buried/ remembered	Haslar Royal Navy Cemetery
Other information	Played football for Audlem. Also played 2nd violin and clarinet in marine band. Awarded long service and good conduct medals.

Sidney Eaton

The biscuits are as hard as rock.
The long trenches drink, but still die.
Instead of delicious cake
there would be hard, dry bread for Sid.
The cakes were calling him home.

The wind rattled like his breath.
The iron burning bees swarmed.
His brothers and sister used to play hide and seek
Now it was his job.

July 1918 – a clear summer air,
But he could not breathe.

Sidney Eaton

Born	April 1894
Enlisted	1915, Smethwick
Died	11 July 1918 in France from pneumonia after recovering from his wounds
Age at death	24
Height	*Not available*
Chest measurements	*Not available*
Job	1911 Apprentice baker
Lived at	Victoria Terrace & Stafford House, Audlem
Father	Stephen Eaton
Mother	Annie
Family	3 brothers, & 1 sister
Regiment	206th siege battery, Royal Garrison Artillery – Gunner 295122
Buried/ remembered	St Sever Cemetery, Rouen, France.
Other information	*Not available*

Albert Ellerton

His life was as peaceful as a monastery, but now his ears are filled with groans, bangs and explosions.
The best village, that all changed since the 14th November 1917.
The bank he lived on was a trench and no more.
At 19 years of life, Watching his friends die was his apprenticeship.

Horrendous food, crunchy cold corned beef, thin, watery soup, and hard dry biscuits.
Field days are the best days, surviving another day, making the most of it.
A boy that led his life, fighting for his country
Letters arriving often, lovely notes and pictures from friends and family members.
Bombs blowing up, men shouting in the intense heat.
His soul fled like a deer fleeing its prey.
Everything left his mind as he fell to the ground, dying in the slop.
The poppies were now his best loving relatives after the horrors of No Man's land and the war.

Albert Ellerton

Born	Oct 1898
Enlisted	Crewe, went to France 16 Oct 1917
Died	14 Nov 1917, Flanders
Age at death	19
Height	*Not available*
Chest measurements	*Not available*
Job	Worked for Mr Goodwin, Monks Farm, Hankelow
Lived at	Chapel End, Cox Bank & 1 Fowl Heath, Audlem
Father	William Henry Ellerton
Mother	Elizabeth Alice Meredith
Family	2 brothers & 2 sisters
Regiment	1st 6th bat Lancashire Fusiliers – Private 47578
Buried/ remembered	Coxyde Military Cemetery, Belgium
Other information	In 1911 census, family of 7 lived in only 3 rooms. Awarded British War & Victory medals

Henry (Harry) Gibson

The food in the trenches reminded him
of the sweets he used to sell.
How he must have thought about his family,
How they must have loved him.

He missed the beautiful trees
swaying in the breeze
and the gritty streets of Crewe.

But his lungs sounded like a train rattling
off the tracks
EGGGHHHH
rolling memories carry on
until the steam washes out.

Henry (Harry) Gibson

Born	Q4 1886
Enlisted	N/A
Died	12 March 1919, bronchial-pneumonia
Age at death	33
Height	*Not available*
Chest measurements	*Not available*
Job	1901 Labourer on farm in Monks Coppenhall, 1911 Confectioner in Manchester
Lived at	1891 - Swanbach; Lawton St Crewe, 18 Thomas St, Rusholme
Father	George Gibson
Mother	Emma
Family	5 brothers, 1 sister
Regiment	1/7th Lancs Fusiliers & 28th company Labour Corps 205206/ 444827 Private
Buried/ remembered	Charleroi Communal Cemetery, Hainaut, Belgium
Other information	*Not available*

In memory of the brave men of this Parish who died for their King and Country in the Great War whose names are recorded on the churchyard cross "lest we forget."

Henry Noel Atkinson D.S.O.	Frederick Griffiths	Ernest Ruscoe
William Bate	Thomas Hampson	Douglas Shuker
Richard Bate	Herbert Hand	Edward Stockton
Leonard Bailey	William Hobson	William Viggars
Clement Beeston	George Lynes	Frank Walker
Ernest William Buckley	John McKenzie	Bertie Whitmore
Haddon Cartwright	Arthur Morrey	George Williams
Herbert Dale	Samuel Morrey	Charles Williams
Albert James Dykes	Arthur Moseley	Frederick Williams
Sidney Eaton	Joseph Neville	George Woolrich
Albert Ellerton	John Thomas Ratcliffe	
Henry Gibson	John Henry Richards	1914–1918
	John Henry Purcell	

The alabaster tablet affixed to the wall in St James Church in Audlem, with the names of 35 men from Audlem who died in the "Great War", 1914-1918. The names are also recorded on the cross in the churchyard (opposite).

Frederick William Griffiths

Born	14 July 1890, Chapel End, Buerton
Enlisted	*Not available*
Died	1914-18
Age at death	24-28
Height	*Not available*
Chest measurements	*Not available*
Job	1911 Farm labourer
Lived at	1891 Cheadle; 1901 Spotland, Rochdale; 1911 Whitworth, Lancs
Father	Frederick
Mother	Elizabeth Ann Roberts
Family	2 sisters, 2 brothers
Regiment	There are 6 possible Fred William Griffiths in various army companies incl 2 in Lancs Fusiliers, but no direct link can be established.
Buried/ remembered	*Not available*
Other information	*Not available*

[Mark Potts]

Thomas Hampson

His lungs were as swollen as a pig
He looked after the animals, now they look after him
He is swimming in his family name
He misses the trees singing and dancing in the wind
He always lived for work, but never this much
He had to slaughter with a mortar
His feet were screaming with pain in muddy dirty water
He nearly survived, but he died at 25.

Thomas Hampson

Born	1893
Enlisted	*Not available*
Died	5 Dec 1918, Prees Heath hospital from pneumonia following influenza
Age at death	25
Height	*Not available*
Chest measurements	*Not available*
Job	Farming at fathers farm
Lived at	Buerton
Father	John Hampson
Mother	Sarah Salmon
Family	1 brother, 2 sisters
Regiment	B bat. 2nd reserve brigade, Royal Field Artillery, 604474 Driver. Also Shropshire Yeomanry & Lancs Fusiliers.
	The Royal Field Artillery was the largest arm of the artillery. It was responsible for the medium calibre guns and howitzers deployed close to the front line and was reasonably mobile. It was organised into brigades, attached to divisions or higher formations. During the first world war a whole new form of artillery was developed to meet the unusual conditions of war on the Western Front: the trench mortar. The Royal Field Artillery provided the manpower for the heavier mortars.
Buried/ remembered	Audlem cemetery, 220, U
Other information	1901, his family employed a domestic servant and a cattle man. 1911, lived on farm with 6 rooms.

Herbert Hand

I fought off dragons, breathing death,
against dreaded flamethrowers.

Our feet are screaming in pain in the trenches.
Rats are as big as cats, biting our numb toes.
The soup is as thick as porridge
same as the jam.

The guns are firing iron burning bees
Stinging people.
Bombs are spitting gas,
and mortars are throwing themselves
into No Man's Land.

The bullets are fearlessly crossing
the Death Trap.
Shrapnel follows me.

Herbert Hand

Born	Q3 1895
Enlisted	Sittingbourne
Died	24 Aug 1916 in France – killed by shrapnel
Age at death	23
Height	*Not available*
Chest measurements	*Not available*
Job	1911 farm labourer
Lived at	Green Lane, Audlem
Father	Lived with Grandfather George, father not named or recorded as present.
Mother	Emma, Grandmother -Mary
Family	None
Regiment	7th bat. Royal Sussex Regiment attached to 130th co. Royal Engineers G/367 Private. "German counter-attacks including flame throwers were beaten off over the next few days, but not without inflicting casualties, especially on 7th Royal Sussex Regiment."
Buried/ remembered	Vermeilles British Cemetery, Pas de Calais, France
Other information	Had earlier been in hospital with the effects of a gas attack.

John Harvey

From Taintree farm
to fields of tainted trees.
The best soldier yet,
of *blazing iron*,
until he died.

And when he died
the day turned grey,
The biscuits were as hard as rock
and the soup ran like men's tears.

John Harvey

Born	3 March 1883 Audlem
Enlisted	*Not available*
Died	20 Sept 1920
Age at death	34
Height	*Not available*
Chest measurements	*Not available*
Job	1911 farm labourer, Hankelow
Lived at	1891 Moblake, Chapel End
	Raines Bank, Audlem
Father	Charles Harvey
Mother	Fanny Broomfield
Family	Married Ethel Edge of Taintree Cottages in 1915.
	1 brother
Regiment	1/5th bat. South Lancashire Regiment,
	32514 Rifleman
Buried/ remembered	Audlem Cemetery, row 28, grave 465
Other information	Fanny remarried after the death of Charles, and so John had 2 half brothers & sister, surname Beech

Frank William Hobson

The rifles are shouting as loud as a metal bell, killing everybody in their way.
Mean tanks tremble momentously, crushing people horrifically.
The savage bayonets are assassinating powerfully.
He misses the trees singing, like a dog misses its owner.
The food is as hard as a rock.

Frank was a *spear*.
He speared moles in the dirt before the war
Now he lives in the mud like the moles he used to catch.
His eyes were as dark as the sea.
And the dirty trenches are drinking quietly.

Frank William Hobson

Born	April 1893, Buerton
Enlisted	12 Nov 1915 at Crewe, together with his friend George Woolrich
Died	1 July 1916, Battle of the Somme
Age at death	23
Height	*Not available*
Chest measurements	*Not available*
Job	1911 mole catcher with his father
Lived at	1901 Chapel End, Buerton
	1911 Long Hill, Hankelow
Father	Frank William
Mother	Mary
Family	2 brothers, 5 sisters
Regiment	17th bat. Manchester Regiment (2nd Manchester Pals) 26433 Private
Buried/ remembered	Dantzig Alley British Cemetery, Mametz, France
Other information	1911, all 10 family members lived in 6 rooms. His friend George Woolrich died on the same day.

It is possible that Frank is pictured on page 96, centre

George Lynes

Audlem was his home town

His new home was as dirty as a pig.

Too young to work,

His college was the vile trenches.

His eyes reflected the wet damp mud.

George Lynes

Born	Audlem 1899
Enlisted	Crewe
Died	25 April 1918 at 4th battle of Ypres, 2nd battle of Kemmel Ridge
Age at death	19
Height	*Not available*
Chest measurements	*Not available*
Job	*Not available*
Lived at	1901 Copthorne, Audlem
	1911 Holly Bank, Audlem
Father	George
Mother	Helen Alice
Family	1 brother 3 sisters. Cousin to Bertie Whitmore who also died.
Regiment	49th bat. Machine Gun Corps – 115352 Private, also 204200 Kings Shropshire Light Infantry
	"In its short history the MGC gained an enviable record for heroism as a front line fighting force. It had a less enviable record for its casualty rate. Some 170,500 officers and men served in the MGC with 62,049 becoming casualties, including 12,498 killed, earning it the nickname 'the Suicide Club'."
Buried/ remembered	Tyne Cot Memorial, Zonnebeke, Belgium.
Other information	His father was granted a war gratuity on 23 Dec 1919.

John Frederick Charles Edmund MacKenzie

The food is as hard as a rock.
The fire bee is flying across No-Man's-Land.
I worried about you.
The trees are screaming as if they are getting set on fire.
The trees are shell shocked as if a soldier was surrounded with bones.
Grassy fields whisper in the breeze,
"John means favoured by God"
The glistening blue sea passes the edge of the rigid rocks.
As the gas is shredding his lungs.

[Owlcation]

John Frederick Charles Edmund MacKenzie

Born	Audlem, 1895
Enlisted	Nantwich, sent to France 22 Dec 1914
Died	4 May 1915, 2nd battle Ypres, battle of St Julien
Age at death	20
Height	*Not available*
Chest measurements	*Not available*
Job	Iron Founder, Railway company
Lived at	1901 Chester Road, Grappenhall; 1911 48 Peel Street, Crewe
Father	John
Mother	Annie
Family	1 brother, 1 sister
Regiment	95th battery, Royal Field Artillery 58575 Acting Bombardier Location: Menin Road/Dumbarton Lakes. Perhaps a German tactical victory, Allies pushed back but Ypres did not fall. Heavy casualties sustained by all combatants. On 22nd April the German Army had launched an offensive (including the use of poisonous gas) driving its perimeter back and creating a break in the line over four miles long. Canadian troops created a series of defensive posts and secured the line. On 24th April, again preceded by a poison gas release, the Germans attacked and despite fierce resistance the Canadian line broke and St Julien fell to the Germans. At the request of the French, British troops staged counter attacks but were forced to withdraw until on 3rd May the Allied lines were only three miles from Ypres. The bitter conflict continued with the Germans taking Frezenberg Ridge, although Allied counter attacks carried on for several more days, incurring heavy casualties.
Buried/ remembered	Menin Gate, Ypres, Belgium
Other information	*Not available*

Arthur Morrey

Arthur Morrey
is an unbreakable rock
in battle. Some of his best friends
got devoured by rats,
bodies strewn on the floor shivering,
drowning.
But Arthur resists.
He is a leader, a *bear-king*,
a brave soldier and most importantly
a friend.

The day he died
Was a dreadful day
a grey day, grey as his eyes.
As grey as Sam's.

Arthur Morrey

Born	Audlem, 1899
Enlisted	12 Sept 1916, Chester
Died	19 Sept 1918
Age at death	19
Height	5' 8"
Chest measurements	35". Weight: 112lbs; scar on left eye from an accident. Hair – brown; complexion – fresh; eyes – grey.
Job	Farm Labourer in 1911
Lived at	1901 Bunsley Bank, then Buerton
Father	Samuel
Mother	Lydia Eliza
Family	1 brother Samuel
Regiment	1/4th bat. Cheshire Regiment, 66591 Private
Buried/ remembered	Tyne Cot Memorial, Belgium
Other information	20 August 1918 Arthur was 'admonished' and docked a day's pay for being absent for a day.
	Went to France on 6 Sept 1918 with expeditionary force, and died only 13 days later.
	On 15 Jan 1920, his father received Arthur's personal effects from the army – 2 discs & a photo card. In Nov 1920, also received a memorial scroll followed by a plaque and his British War and Victory medals.
	Brother Samuel also died, but in 1915.

Samuel Morrey

Born with a scar, like he was meant to fight.
The bullets are like stinging bees.
Green crops growing turned into blown-up soil
Only God would know what would happen
and who will die.

His eyes were dead trees.
And the food had rotted for months.
He lay frozen like a block of ice.
Samuel, *God healed,*
But not this time.

Samuel Morrey

Born	Oct 1893, Audlem
Enlisted	Sent to France 22 May 1915
Died	25 Sept 1915 in 2nd attack on Bellewaarde, Belgium
Age at death	21
Height	*Not available*
Chest measurements	*Not available*
Job	Farm Labourer. 1911 worked for William Ernest Bowie at College Fields as a cowman.
Lived at	1901 Bunsley Bank, 1911 Buerton
Father	Samuel
Mother	Lydia Eliza
Family	1 brother Arthur
Regiment	5th bat. Kings Shropshire Light Infantry, 11197 Private
Buried/ remembered	Menin Gate, Ypres, Belgium
Other information	Brother of Arthur who was killed in 1918

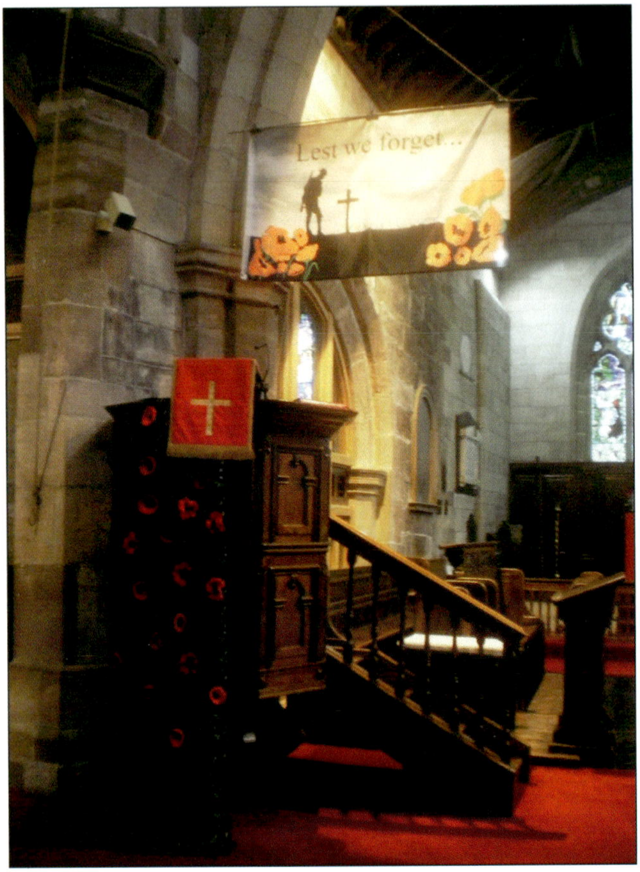
Lest we forget...

Arthur Levi Watkin Moseley

Born	5 Feb 1892 Audlem; baptised 6 March 1892
Enlisted	11 Nov 1914
Died	9 Aug 1918, France
Age at death	26
Height	5'8"
Chest measurements	37". Complexion: fair; eyes: grey; hair: brown
Job	Auctioneers' Clerk
Lived at	1901 Hankelow;
	1911 Stags Head pub, Market Drayton
Father	Charles – Innkeeper in 1911
Mother	Adeline Fanny from Widnes
Family	3 brothers
Regiment	29th bat. Canadian Infantry (Vancouver), 75201 Company Sergeant Major; before he had served in Kings Shropshire Light Infantry for 2.5 years.
Buried/ remembered	Rosieres Communal Cemetery, Somme, France
Other information	Arthur age 20 departed from Liverpool on vessel Empress of Ireland. Arrived 13 May 1912 in Quebec Canada.
	Killed in the morning of 9 Aug 1918 when a shell fell close by, when advancing towards Rosiére.

Joseph Neville

Joseph Neville

Born	1893 Audlem
Enlisted	8 Sept 1914, went to France 14th July 1915.
Died	29 May 1919 in Audlem
Age at death	26
Height	5' 9"
Chest measurements	35"; weight 136lbs; complexion – fresh; hair – brown; eyes – grey.
Job	1911 Groom for Arthur Spragg Hocknell at New Town, Audlem
Lived at	1901 -Wilkesley Cottage; Mayfield Cottage, Heywood Lane, Audlem
Father	Joseph Edward
Mother	Sarah Jane Worrall
Family	3 brothers, 1 sister
Regiment	No 2 depot, Royal Field Artillery, 19230 Driver; then 1 May 1915 posted to Ammunition Column, 8th Reserve Brigade.
Buried/ remembered	Audlem row, 32 grave 545.
Other information	Discharged as medically unfit 12 March 1917 after suffering shell shock in May 1916. Badly gassed at the front, suffered badly from its effects and never recovered. His brother Harry Bert survived the war having joined in Nov 1915, and was discharged on 20 May 1920. His funeral was conducted by Rev J.W Goddard Rector of Adderley in the absence of the Vicar.

John Henry Purcell

He was a giant in the trenches that could barely stand up.
His eyes were bright blue like a swimming pool ready to be swum in.
The people around town are now just bodies, lying dead on
the wet, muddy ground.
All his books never prepared him for No Man's Land.

His father was always proud of him.
He looks for his brothers and sisters in the trenches,
but they are hiding and seeking at home.
His lungs stopped taking in the autumn air.

But dying at 22, he won't remember much.

John Henry Purcell

Born	21 Feb 1892 Audlem
Enlisted	Undertook medical at Carmarthen, 2 Nov 2016. Records show enlisted Hereford 19 March 1917
Died	1 Oct 1918 in Mesopotamia (Iran).
Age at death	22
Height	5'6"
Chest measurements	34"
Job	Bookstall clerk, 1911 Grocer
Lived at	1901 Paddock Lane, Audlem; 1911 Bridge House, Swanbach
Father	John from Cradley near Malvern
Mother	Minnie Jones
Family	6 sisters and 3 brothers
Regiment	730th M.T. Company, Army Service Corps, M/301686 Private. Trained at Grove Park March 1917. Soldiers who served in the Mechanical Transport usually had the letter M as a prefix to their number. Those in the Lines of Communication operated in a wide variety of roles, such as being attached to the heavy artillery as Ammunition Columns or Parks, being Omnibus Companies, Motor Ambulance Convoys, or Bridging and Pontoon units.
Buried/ remembered	Tehran War Cemetery, Iran; St James Church, Malvern, war memorial
Other information	Was a Wesleyan Methodist. On 29 April 1917, travelled to Durban and Bombay. On his arrival in India he was posted to a Reinforcement Camp where he was employed on "general camp duties." He re-embarked on the Transport Ship Empress of Britain for Bombay, from where he changed ships and sailed on the HT Elephanta bound for Basra in Mesopotamia (modern day Iraq). Here he was posted to 730 MT Coy on 28th August as a Ford motor driver.

On 27 January 1918 he joined the Dunsterville Column at Baghdad, which was mounting a force into South Russia to stem the Russian Revolution.

Admitted to hospital in Kasvin in June, and died of pneumonia. Memorial scroll and King's letter sent to his father in 1920.

John Thomas Ratcliffe

The groans of the cows soon became the groans of soldiers.

He was so used to nice food, but now it is just sloppy old soup.

He was so used to fields of flowers, now all he sees is fields of dead people.

John Thomas Ratcliffe

Born	Q3 1890, Burleydam
Enlisted	20 Jan 1917 Whitchurch, sent to France 19 June 1917.
Died	8 Sept 1917, Belgium
Age at death	27
Height	5' 4"
Chest measurements	37.5"; weight: 138lbs
Job	Cow man
Lived at	Ightfield Hall, Whitchurch & Mob Lake, Buerton
Father	John
Mother	Charlotte, née Evans
Family	Wife: Elsie May, née Ellison, married June 1917. She married again after the war and became 'Glassey'. His daughter Doris M Ratcliffe Glassey born in Dec 1917 after he had died. He also had 2 brothers, 1 sister.
Regiment	75th company, Machine Gun Corps, 97570 Private. Formerly Kings Shropshire Light Infantry, 293572
Buried/ remembered	Mendinghem Military cemetery, Belgium
Other information	Character on military record 'good'. Died of gunshot wound to the head. Elsie May received his medals 30 Aug 1922 and memorial scroll, 13 Feb 1918.

John Henry Richards

John Richards, "beloved" "brave ruler".

The whistles signified his death.

His deep blue oceans flooded onto burnt sand

And the shrapnel burned as fast as a racing tiger.

The biscuits are as hard as steel,

Burning fire-bees drift towards him.

Guns are screaming, bringing DEATH with every shot.

He sits like a rocking chair in the corner of the trench.

John Henry Richards

Born	Q4 1895, Adderley
Enlisted	Shrewsbury
Died	24 April 1918 in King George's Hospital, London
Age at death	23
Height	*Not available*
Chest measurements	*Not available*
Job	Railway porter
Lived at	1901 Stafford St, Audlem,
	1911 Station View, Audlem
Father	William – stationmaster at Audlem
Mother	Annie Shuker
Family	3 brothers, 1 sister
Regiment	Royal Field Artillery, 169192 Gunner
Buried/ remembered	St Peters Church, Thundersley, Essex.
Other information	Member of Audlem church choir.
	1911 - 5 family members + 3 boarders lived in 6 rooms.
	Wounded in the head by shrapnel, 26 Oct 1917, taken to King George's Hospital, London, 21 Nov 1917.

Ernest Ruscoe

My food is bitter and hard as the ground,
The metal bees are killing my *mateys*,
My little darlings are probably dreaming about me.

Vicious guns devour menacingly,
Ernest is as still as a frozen block of ice,
Only God knows who will go and who will stay.

If I die, I want to tell you that I love you
so much, but the guns
are as fierce as tigers.

Ernest Ruscoe

Born	1897, Tunstall
Enlisted	Shrewsbury, went to France 24 July 1915
Died	12 Feb 1916, Ypres, Belgium
Age at death	19
Height	*Not available*
Chest measurements	*Not available*
Job	1911 - waggoner
Lived at	1901 - Spoonby Rd, Adderley;
	1911 - 5 Wood St, Hadnall, Shropshire.
Father	Joseph
Mother	Eliza Ann
Family	4 brothers, 2 sisters - some of them were born in Audlem
Regiment	6th bat. Kings Shropshire Light Infantry, 12433 Lance Corporal
Buried/ remembered	Artillery Wood Cemetery, Ypres, Belgium
Other information	1911, all 10 family members lived in 4 rooms.

[Mark Potts]

(Lying, far right) [Mark Potts]

Douglas Shuker

The biscuits are as hard as iron.
The burning bees are shouted out of the mouths of the guns,
his feet are burning in lava.
His uniform is waiting for him.
There are vicious rats in the horrible, muddy trenches
He is black steam too dark to see. His eyes are as gloomy a s the trenches,
As he thinks
I miss my family so much, yet, we can't talk.

Douglas Shuker

Born	July 1894
Enlisted	Dec 1915, London
Died	1 July 1916 Gommecourt; 1st day Battle of the Somme. (19,000 soldiers were killed on 1st day.)
Age at death	22
Height	*Not available*
Chest measurements	*Not available*
Job	1911 Apprentice (Assistant Clothier) to Mr Wood – Gents Outfitter, Market Drayton, then for Peter Robinson in London
Lived at	Woodside, Cox Bank Audlem
Father	Frederick John
Mother	Hannah
Family	1 sister, 1 brother
Regiment	1/14th bat. London Regiment (London Scottish); 512439, Private
Buried/ remembered	Gommecourt British Cemetery, No 2 Hebuterne, Pas de Calais, France
Other information	16 July 1916 the family received a 'missing in action, presumed dead' letter.

Arthur Smith

Arthur Smith

Born	11 Sept 1896, Audlem
Enlisted	Served in France, Belgium and Germany
Died	29 Oct 1920
Age at death	24
Height	*Not available*
Chest measurements	*Not available*
Job	Railway, members of NUR attended his funeral
Lived at	Copthorne, Audlem
Father	James
Mother	Jane
Family	4 brothers, 1 sister
Regiment	Royal Garrison Artillery 160953 Gunner
Buried/ remembered	Audlem Cemetery, row 28 grave 473
Other information	He was badly gassed and was in a sanatorium for 4 months prior to his death.
	His funeral service conducted by A.V.C Hordern, pall bearers J Tapley, Jos. Morrey, Thomas Tatler, A Rickard, T.W Green and F Hand. 'There was a large number of wreaths'.

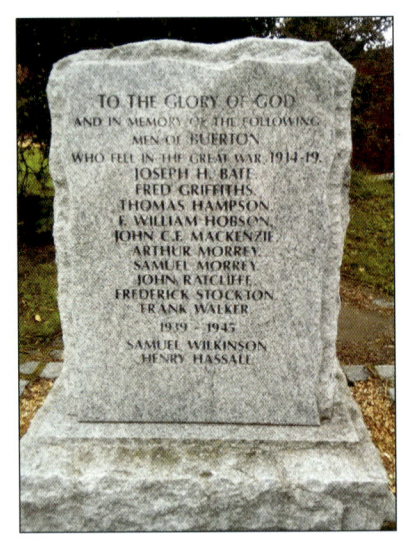

Buerton War Memorial includes
Stockton's name

(Frederick) Edward Stockton

Sharp guns are shouting meanly
AND SPITTING OUT FIRE.
Our feet are screaming with pain in muddy WATER.
In the dirt of No Man's Land,
The rats are as big as cats.
I USED TO HEAR COWS MOOING IN
THE FIELD,
Now only the groans of injured soldiers.
I imagine the chestnuts dancing in the wind
In my home town of Buerton.

(Frederick) Edward Stockton

The birth certificate is registered as Frederick, but it is believed that Edward and Frederick were both names he used. He appears as Edward on electoral rolls but Frederick on census returns and it is this name he enlisted under as well. This assumption has been made based on the age of both names being the same.
Frederick is the name on Buerton War Memorial.

Born	Q4 1882 Buerton
Enlisted	Crewe
Died	'On or since' 1 Aug 1917, 'presumed dead,' E.g. body never found. 3rd battle of Ypres, Passchendaele.
Age at death	33
Height	*Not available*
Chest measurements	*Not available*
Job	1901 (Frederick) Grocers horse man, 1911 (Edward) Wagoner on farm
Lived at	1891 (Frederick) scholar. 1905-1915 Chapel End Buerton, appears on electoral roll every year as Edward
Father	Joseph Stockton
Mother	Annie Griffiths
Family	4 brothers 2 sisters
Regiment	16th (Service) Bat Welsh Regiment Private 54392
Buried/ remembered	Menin Gate Ypres Belgium, bay 37, stone L.
Other information	Left his 'soldiers effects' divided between his brothers and sisters; 16 shillings 6 pence each, + further £4, 10 shillings given to brother Joseph 5 months later.

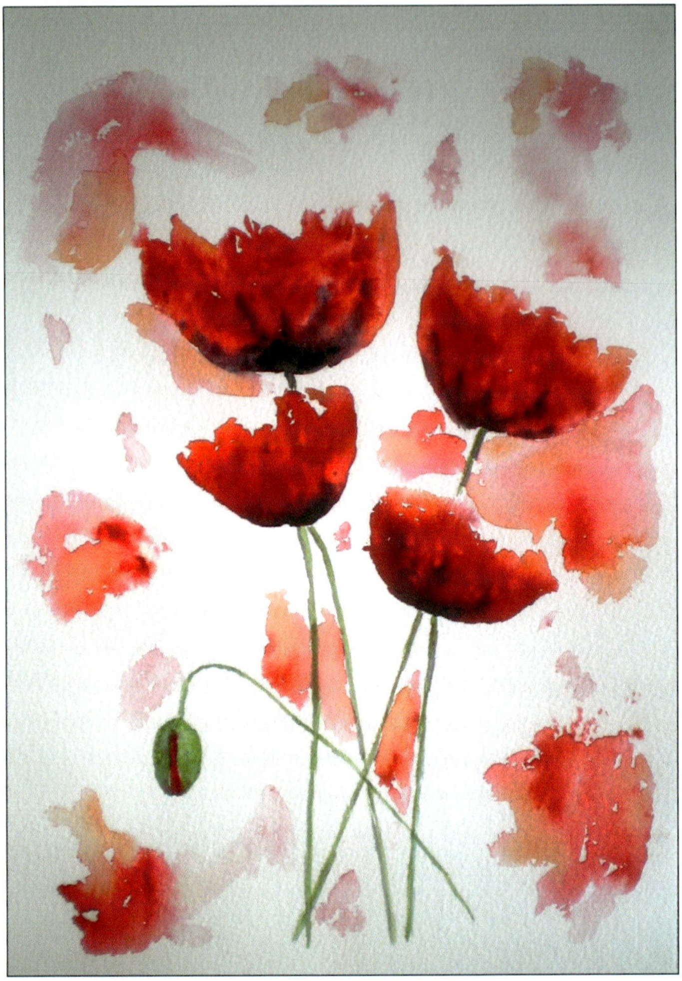

Richard William Viggars

Born	March 1892, Audlem
Enlisted	Crewe; arrived in Boulogne 6 Nov 1915
Died	1 July 1916 Montauban, 1st day of the Battle of the Somme
Age at death	24
Height	*Not available*
Chest measurements	*Not available*
Job	*Not available*
Lived at	1901 Stocktons Cottage, Newhall; 1911 Rope Bank, Audlem
Father	Alfred
Mother	Mary Ann
Family	4 brothers, 2 sisters
Regiment	17th (Service) bat. Manchester Regiment; (2nd Manchester Pals); 26435 Private
Buried/ remembered	Thiepval Memorial, Somme, France.
Other information	*Not available*

Frank Walker

Too young to work,
my apprenticeship
is seeing my friends die at war.
All of us are dancing to our death
but I hope it isn't me today.

My wife is in bed
my little duckies are in my head
their eyes as blue as the *Skye*.
Probably sleeping now
dreaming about me as I dream about them.

Metal bees are killing all my mates,
Golden bees stinging the brave men.

The bread is as hard as a ROCK.
All of us men are shivering
like jelly on a plate
shivering so much
we would fall off the spoon.
Pud has turned into mud.
Some men are awarded medals for bravery and courage.
Not for me, but still I fought off dragons breathing death.
.

My lovely food has turned into dust.
The cakes at home are calling my name.

The planes are evil birds
dropping their eggs
and unfortunately
one has landed on me.

Frank Walker

Born	Jan 1899, Adderley
Enlisted	12 Sept 1916, Chester, went to Le Havre 2 March 1917
Died	16 April 1917, France. Killed with 3 others by a bomb dropped from an aeroplane.
Age at death	18
Height	*Not available*
Chest measurements	*Not available*
Job	*Not available*
Lived at	1901 Adderley; 1911 Buerton; Kynsal Heath, Audlem
Father	George Slaney Walker
Mother	Jessie May Morrey
Family	3 brothers, 4 sisters
Regiment	3rd/5th bat. Lancashire Fusiliers, 203243 Private
Buried/ remembered	Bethune Town Cemetery, Pas de Calais, France
Other information	In 1911 - 11 members of family lived in 6 rooms.

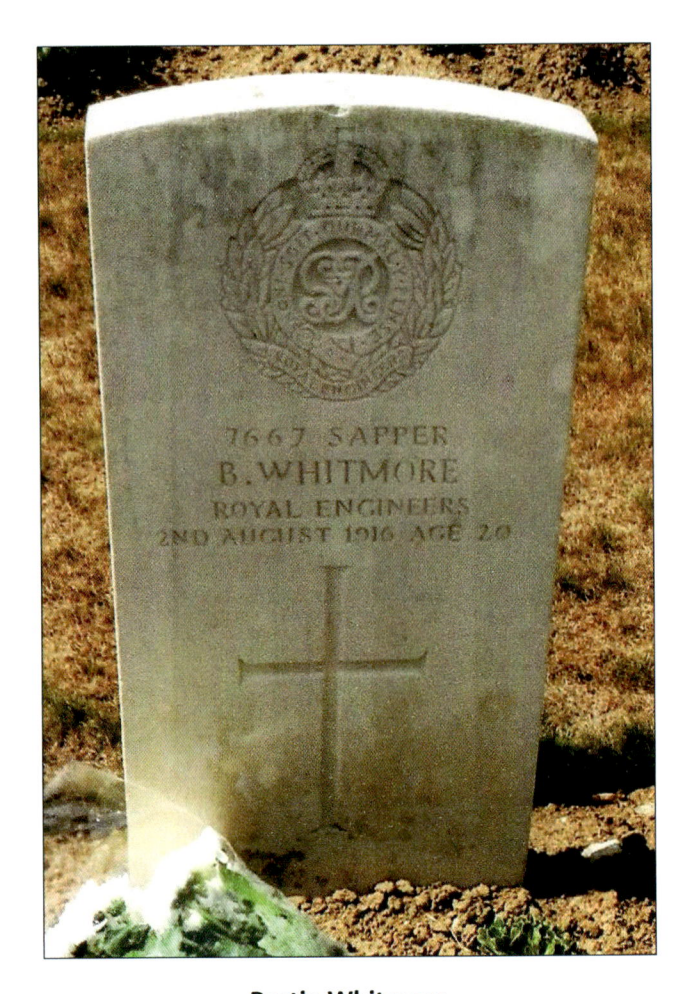

Bertie Whitmore

Bertie Whitmore

Born	30 May 1896, Lock House, Audlem
Enlisted	7 May 1915, Crewe, sent to France 6 Oct 1915
Died	2 Aug 1916, Battle of the Somme
Age at death	20
Height	N/A
Chest measurements	N/A
Job	N/A
Lived at	1901 Lock House Swanbach; 1911 Canal Side, Audlem.
Father	No father named on birth certificate. Grandfather - John
Mother	Frances Emma Whitmore; Drapers assistant. Grandmother – Emma Toy
Family	Cousin of George Lynes who also died
Regiment	2nd siege co, Royal Engineers, 7667, Sapper.
Buried/ remembered	Mailly-Maillet Communal Cemetery extension, Somme, France
Other information	Killed by shrapnel whilst carrying material along the trenches.

Charles Albert Williams

Charles Albert Williams

Born	1899 Shropshire
Enlisted	July 1918, Prees Heath, Shropshire
Died	9 Oct 1918 at Prees Heath Camp
Age at death	19
Height	*Not available*
Chest measurements	*Not available*
Job	Apprentice to W Sheen, Grocer, Audlem
Lived at	1911 Kynsal Heath; 1918 Stable Yard, Adderley
Father	(John) Lloyd – gentleman farmer
Mother	Mary
Family	9 brothers and sisters
Regiment	21st Bat. 49th Training Reserve Kings Liverpool Regiment; TR3/72647 Private
Buried/ remembered	Audlem Cemetery, row 26 grave 428
Other information	Regular attendee at St James, member of choir and young men's Bible class. Charles visited his home on Sunday and complained of feeling heavy and chest pains. He cycled back to Prees Camp that evening in the pouring rain. On Tuesday he went into hospital and died the next day at 11am before his parents could see him. He had a bright and cheerful disposition and was well liked. His body was escorted from camp to Whitchurch station by the military. Pall bearers J Hamnett, C Shuker, A Timmis, L. Cadman.

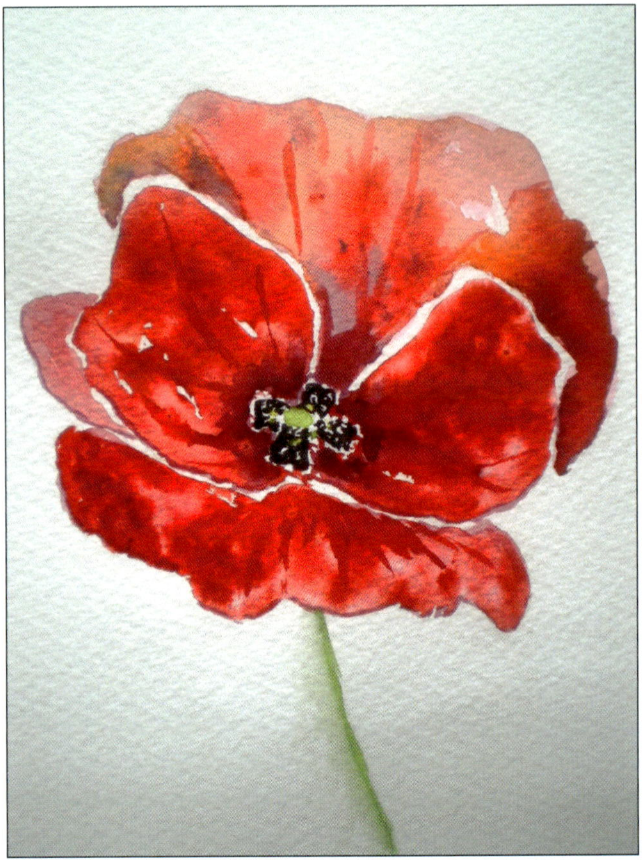

Frederick Williams

Born	1899 Coole Pilate, baptised 14 March 1900 in Acton
Enlisted	Crewe
Died	1 Sept 1918, France
Age at death	19
Height	*Not available*
Chest measurements	*Not available*
Job	Grocer for J Wood Audlem, also worked at Cooperative Society, Audlem
Lived at	1901 Coole Pilate, 1911 Church Fields, Audlem
Father	Joseph
Mother	Ellen
Family	No
Regiment	1/3rd (City of London) bat. Royal Fusiliers; 80523 Private. Formerly 24745 1st (Reserve) Cavalry Regiment.
Buried/ remembered	Sailly-Saillisel British Cemetery, Somme, France
Other information	*Not available*

[Stephen Benson, www.cheshireroll.co.uk]

George Watkin Williams

George Watkin Williams

Born	Q1 1895
Enlisted	Shrewsbury
Died	26 April 1917, Battle of Arras
Age at death	22
Height	*Not available*
Chest measurements	*Not available*
Job	1911 Draper's apprentice; Assistant at Stretch and Harlock, Nantwich
Lived at	1901 at Bridge Inn, Audlem, with both parents; 1911 at Bridge Inn, with step father, and mother
Father	George Williams
Mother	Gertrude B. Kendall – remarried name; née Watkin
Family	1 brother, 1 sister, 1 half brother, 1 half sister
Regiment	7th (Service) bat. Kings Shropshire Light Infantry, 26703 Private. Formerly 2314 Shropshire Yeomanry
Buried/ remembered	Arras Memorial, Pas de Calais, France
Other information	As a boy, a prominent member of Audlem Parish Church choir. He was the 3rd member of the choir to die, 6 others were wounded.

Fred Woodbine

Fred Woodbine

Born	1886 Middlewich
Enlisted	1914
Died	6 Aug 1920
Age at death	34
Height	N/A
Chest measurements	N/A
Job	1911 butcher/ Slaughterer. Member of NUR.
Lived at	1901 & 1911 -55 Chester Road, Middlewich. On Electoral role 1920 at 6 Stafford Street, Audlem
Father	James
Mother	Sarah Ellen Downing
Family	Married Annie E Green, Q2 1918 Nantwich 3 brothers, 3 sisters
Regiment	3rd bat. East Lancs regiment, 17462 Private
Buried/ remembered	Audlem Cemetery, row 27, grave 453
Other information	Wounded twice and badly gassed. Awarded the Victory & British medals in April 1919.

(on right)
[Mark Potts]

George Thomas Woolrich

The water is as an ice block and the bottle is as muddy as their clothes.
The worn out trenches sleep scorched by the bombs, scared they will stir
once again.
The poor, spotty, dog is falling in pain.
The old tanks are stomping in anger.
His face used to be black with the smoke
of his workshop. Now it is black with mud.
He misses how his hammer used to sing
against the metal.
Now, his toe is the only hammer he has left.

George Thomas Woolrich

Born	1896, Hankelow
Enlisted	Woolwich - Nov 1915 discharged 'not likely to be an efficient soldier'. Crewe Nov 1915 with Frank Hobson
Died	1 July 1916, Battle of the Somme attacking Montauban
Age at death	20
Height	5' 6"
Chest measurements	35". Hammer toe on left foot.
Job	Blacksmith's Apprentice with his father
Lived at	1901 & 1911, Hankelow; 1915, 33 Mitford Street, Stretford
Father	Thomas
Mother	Emily Susan
Family	3 sisters
Regiment	'D' Company, 17th (Service) bat. Manchester Regiment, (2nd Manchester Pals); 26434 Private
Buried/ remembered	Thiepval Memorial, Somme, France
Other information	Died on same day as his friend Frank Hobson

Thank you

ALL WHO SERVED, SACRIFICED, AND CHANGED OUR WORLD

1918 - 2018